Open these covers! Inside you'll find abundant evidence of Franklin K.R. Cline's quicksilver intelligence, in apparently conversational poems that if attended well, reveal a singular ear/mind for fellow wisdom, a fine respite/shelter in the current moment.

—Karl Gartung

Cline, Franklin K.R. *The Beatles' Second Album.*

First Edition. November, 2021

Library of Congress Control Number: 2021950210

ISBN: 978-1-952055-39-3

front cover art by MJ

front and back cover photography by Franklin K.R. Cline on an iphone 10

THE BEATLES' SECOND ALBUM

POEMS BY FRANKLIN K.R. CLINE

for john and clint

It seemed that in spite of all his wrong-doing, weakness, guilt—in spite of his humanity—he was getting another chance. There was no accounting for one's good fortune, that was plain. There it simply was, taking his elbow in its hand.

—Salman Rushdie, *The Satanic Verses*

the only thing to do is simply continue
is that simple
yes, it is simple because it is the only thing to do
can you do it
yes, you can because it is the only thing to do

—Frank O'Hara, "Adieu to Norman, Bonjour to Joan and Jean-Paul"

THE NATIONAL ANTHEM

Regularly shit gets blown prettily up
    when whoever's singing sings the word *glare*, which is the rocket's,
to punctuate the violence, or

defamiliarize it, I'm not
    sure. Sometimes I go to the grocery store
and just walk around when I'm feeling lonely. The rockets

and bombs *gave proof,* the song says:
    violence was our best option, and despite and/or because of the kabooms,
the flag remained. I expect people to be there

for me all the time but I am terrible
    at reciprocating, at
listening. Outside of Matt and Aly's Chicago garden apartment

the city erected
    a massive flag that warbles pathetically; it's too colossal
for the soft breezes

of the Windy City. Matt hypothesizes it's
    so you can see the flag from your car,
going east on I-90. If I had any empathy for this broken country, I would hurtle it

at this flag, the inadvertent piteousness of itself wrapped around itself,
nowhere
    to go but further inward. On still days, you can't
even really tell what it is other than a mélange

of red
    approximating blood and blue
approximating sky.

DEATH

FRANKLIN K.R. CLINE WALKS INTO A BAR
sonnet for klingers east

and it kicks ass! bars rule
cant swing my dick without hitting a bar in milwaukee

love to sit on a stool and find myself
chatting with whoever amongst

miniature fanfare for the brewers game
the crossword in todays paper

passed around. who got
the next round? ah,

thanks i got the next one
four five six of us sittin around

each buys two rounds im no
mathematician but thats eight drinks

amongst the four five six of us in an hour snow falls
we stumble home showered in it

TELEVISION

it is bright and shining down on
me in the uncomfortable bed in
which i am maybe dying the
chiefs are playing and it is
snowing on the television i
cannot see outside it is maybe
snowing in kansas city or
perhaps they are in denver
either way i am confident the
chiefs will win although i
cannot really follow it mostly i
watch people cook in
competition which is strange
because it seems the idea
behind food is that of
convergence and togetherness
but they seem to be trying to
make dishes that are better
than the others under a time
constraint to be honest they all
look good i wonder what it
would be like if they just all
worked together and made one
big nice dish i dont understand
why everyone is competing i
watch a lot of b.e.t. in the
mornings because martin is
funny and theres really nothing
else on other than the sports
men yelling at each other and
south park and i dont really
care for either i should watch
the news but i cant quite follow
it i need something very comic
and easy and swallowable plus i
just want the soothing light to
come and shine on me and
make me feel normal yes i cant

eat much they bring me a menu
but i cant eat most of it because
of some dietary restrictions that
confuse me but are probably
very simple so whatever i call
them sometimes at 2 am to get
a cup of ice cream or cold water
because i am parched and tired
and i leave the tv on all the time
usually espn at night i like scott
van pelt i like sportscenter i
watched the dodgers win the
world series and talked with a
custodian whose niece moved
to la she was very happy for her
niece so i was happy for her to
be happy for her niece baseball
is a great thing to watch when
you cant move because it is
slow and steady and it makes
you feel like you are not dying
when you are dying guy fieri
also does not get his due he is
extremely comforting because
it does seem as though he
genuinely appreciates life at its
fullest although i would not ask
him to speak at my funeral i
should write him a letter and
see if he will visit me in the
hospital after all he has some
restaurant somewhere in the
power and light district i went
there once with walter i got the
trash can nachos they were not
served on the lid of a trash can
which i found disappointing i
bet i drank in secret before i
saw walter little bottles on the

bus sometimes i use memory
like a television and i gotta say i
did not live a show i would
want to watch

FRANKLIN K.R. CLINE WALKS INTO A BAR
sonnet with a line from the young rascals

ah everyone digging it having fun we are full of and
out of love and *groovin*

on a sunday afternoon the cool bar
next to the acupuncture place

have a few and maybe a shot
or two with the bartender who doesnt

know the depths of your addiction! whoa
this shit is gonna kill you dude

this shit is gonna kill you dude
your veins will be so visible

your body is an unwatered plant but
you are not a cactus man you cant

just live this kind of wet life drink water
remember nmi wiconi

AIRPORTS

where lots of people go to
go somewhere else for
whatever reasons some
people at airports seem so
sad some so hopeful most
lonely some excited it is like
a hospital in that way you
can see the faces drooping
amongst espn if youre lucky
and fox news if youre not at
least airports sell booze i
guess you could sneak
booze into a hospital would
probably be pretty easy you
cant bring a gun into an
airport but if you really
wanted to you could
enough to do some damage
god please do not do that
please do not harm anyone
other than yourself and
even then only harm
yourself to the extent to
which it will not harm
anyone else who loves you
do you believe in love have
you been loved or ever
loved it is okay to say no it
is okay to not experience
that i for instance will never
go to maccu picchu so
maybe in some way i have
never been in love either i
do not like airports wait
thats not true i like airports
i do not like airplanes i do
not like going up into the
sky *indian* i always say

16

jokingly *we like the ground*
but of course you know the
ground aint ours much
anymore the sky once was
maybe but now it is for
planes and clouds and
shades that toby told me
werent visible during the
grecian empire toby said to
me over a subway sandwich
climate change has changed
the color of the sky and
homer's wine-dark sea is not
something something who
cares sorry toby who we
once were airports are a
chance to be nobody i like
being nobody i love to be
anonymous but i also love
to be recognized amongst
the small puddle of my
friends the beers are too
expensive in airports it is a
strange captivity the food is
too expensive and also not
very good i am tired and
hungry even though i just
ate a tuna salad sandwich
we made sunday so the
tuna was going to go bad
and i should just make
another one to save money
but the one i had was not
very good and i dont want
another this is a problem
with earth this is why we go
into the sky right to get
away from the mundane
however briefly to be

anonymous is either
comforting or terrifying but
one thing we do on an
airplane is hope we land
alive which is a we not an i

FRANKLIN K.R. CLINE WALKS INTO A BAR
sonnet with a line from Philip Larkin

and it is whatever in the middle of the whatever

                    who knows anymore when

                              who knows

everyone is texting asking where you are and who knows

          somewhere maybe the uptowner playing pinball although

you dont have cash so that doesnt seem right there is

a pinball machine there though so you cant be too far off

the trees are turning into leaf like something almost being said

                  what are you saying something almost

      what are you saying what is coming out of your mouth

what is going to happen to your body to you to anything

to the crunch of the homeward stop

wasnt it just snowing how are there leaves on the ground

           what the fuck is going on with
           time

SPORTS

ah shit i remember when the chiefs
drafted patrick mahomes i was
already drunk before siwars thing i
was watching the nfl draft the chiefs
traded up 17 picks to get the man
out of texas tech the unproven qb
patrick mahomes i was taking a shit
and my ex wife said *hey* i figured
she was just saying something
unimportant which is why she is my
ex wife but anyway she said *hey* and
then i went out of the bathroom and
they announced the trade and with
the tenth pick in the draft the
kansas city chiefs select a
quarterback out of texas tech
patrick mahomes the second and i
had won some money off of a game
he played against the sooners
where id bet the over and it hit like
in the third quarter and i thought ok
cool this dude is good anyway who
cares i love sports they are a small
microcosm of life insamuch as there
are always winners and losers and
yes i do not believe in binaries but
at the same time i suppose i sort of
do so that makes me either a piece
of shit or not i mean i am a piece of
shit figuratively sports are so fun
you can watch baseball during the
day and back when i drank it was a
great excuse to get fucked up it still
is a great excuse to get fucked up
and god bless all the people who do
i hope they have one for me in my
honor the royals might win
something like 80 games this

year one hopes that would be cool
they werent very good for awhile
after they won the big one but who
is the thunder have lost like 15
straight it sucks they are obviously
not good they are openly tanking as
its called which means they are just
fucking up to fuck up so they get
maybe a better draft pick in the
lottery but the lottery is rigged so i
suppose capitalism works in some
fashion in the hospital i watched a
lot of espn because it was on all the
time and there were a lot of college
football games i did not care about
the chiefs won the two games they
played when i was hospitalized and
then they were off which was nice i
wanted to be off too why do we
desire sports so badly why do we
want to see the people we root for
win why do we root for anyone
other than ourselves in the first
place why does geographical
location determine the teams for
whom we root anyway unless you
are young and then its just the best
team like i liked the 49ers when i
was a kid because they had steve
young or whatever and were very
good so i liked them i even had a
hat of theirs from where i don't
know probably walmart why does
microsoft word capitalize walmart
why do we capitalize anything it is
all capital i suppose anyway the
teams i root for are mine and
mine alone

FRANKLIN K.R. CLINE WALKS INTO A BAR
sonnet

ah the dj is dropping some hotness
you go to see a gal you like who invited you out but shes on a date
he offers you some weed you smoke it on the dance floor
then you rap the first verse of gin and juice to yourself
and you go get a beer and a shot you go back to the dance floor
the dj plays flava in your ear (remix) you dance a bit quietly alone
it is real nice to be alone in retrospect though at the time
you will want to badly to be with anyone
you want so badly to be with anyone you transform yourself
into another person so you can be with him
so youre never really alone
youre with this other you all the time too
the next day your therapist tells you *when the sadness comes let it in*
invite it to sit with you on the couch and talk to it

TO BE

never thought id really get over it, never thought
anyone would ever
i mean after i mean

theres so much patience required with me its like im a hospital

im getting spontaneous nosebleeds which ive never had before because my soul
isnt right and so its manifesting itself out of my nose and into my shirt

im leaving blood on olivias bedsheets

my veins are visible
my veins are visible
my veins are visible
my veins are visible

i always think about the sky cause i look at the sky as often as i can but right now i
feel so kept indoors that i didnt even know it was raining until it was done raining
and even then i didnt know until someone told me it had rained i feel so unaware
of the earth so floaty and disembodied i dont really know how to handle it

i always recycle but that doesnt fix any problems

my veins are visible
my veins are visible
my veins are visible
my veins are visible

i used a plastic fork to eat a taco out of a styrofoam container

i do not feel good about being on the planet and i do not really understand how to
remedy that. there's probably a book that would help and i want to go smoke dope
but even now dope just makes me itchy and hyper

i have nowhere to go but up
i have nowhere to go but in
i have nowhere to go
my veins are visible just like my fathers

franklin k.r. cline walks into a bar
by mikey swanberg (of good grief [VA-55] and on earth as it is [VA-86] fame)

& with me behind him
& with me with both hands
in his ass pockets like the back
of a horse in a horse costume we forgot

& anyway there we are
shooting the shit okay
& shooting pool real bad
pissing into the same tub
while our burgers sizzle up

& buying a round & rough housing
& the house is in rough shape
franklin says

he is about to move
but likes his neighbors   likes the piles
of shoes on the landing heading upstairs

& i always liked the smell of a foot
or got so used to it anyway
i couldn't start caring   the body   the body
what can you say   we are alive
for a time & get to stink
to high heaven   get to get high
before the reading

& there goes the name
of the former milwaukee poet laureate
right out of my head   blowing
past the docks and into the lake
as free as a 99¢ cheetos bag
& at least as lovely

this is what ive been working on
said the artist to me and franklin
standing in his studio looking at his paintings
well this is what ive been trying to work on
& anyway thanks for coming

MAYBE

CITIZEN

what does it mean
to be a citizen

what does it mean
to be a good person

i ate wings today with paul

we went together there in a car

lets build a big old bridge
and all walk across it

if the world ended today would you love me

COME WANDER WITH ME
sestina

reader, im bored
the cars
are racing by out
on the big prismatic
post-rain highway made out of
concrete or asphalt the cars roar past in green

outside spring the green
leaves are boredly
flapping around out of
their minds the cars
similarly their prismatic
wheels glinting in the post-rain drought

those speeding who ought
have left earlier the road a whole big green
light to keep going no prismatic
stoplight here theyre not bored
the drivers of the cars not the cars
themselves which are made of

uh i dont know what a car is made of
steel and bolts im not sure whats on the outside aluminum i dont know much about cars
the leaves are the green
of a pool table or a dartboard
i am always aiming poorly at the prismatic

spread of lifes dartboard my prismatic
spray of darts of-
ten off the board
an inch or so out
far away from the green
come to think of it the 1993 geo prizm, my first car

my car
the geo prizm

30

shined in kansas city and kirksville in a lived-in mint green
i am so much love
i am out
of energy im happy i was on the board

of directors at woodland pattern spring is dragging itself into the city
greening the cars
how could i be bored amongst all this prismatic
life of which i do not want out

A LOVE SUPREME
sonnet

seven hits in the ninth
a person at the bar squiggly
asking to turn off the coltrane to get
the announcers on and a person
agreeing another person
with sunglasses all existing in the type
of day that makes everyone want to be

alive coltrane squiggling his way towards
truth wow they strung together six in the ninth to tie
it up it must be the way the grass
is cut the music
bumps a runner home as a fan
id like the announcers i like the music why cant we have both

AT LEAST WE SHOWED UP
sonnet for 3305a n pierce st

freddy ordered pizza from lisas

we watched natural born killers and smoked cigarettes

theres so much to say for having been there

how can you make a clean break with your life

i feel the need to lecture you here
but you already read poetry   you get it

in natural born killers they kill an indian and then say
theyll never kill again but then they kill
robert downey jrs character who does have it coming

recently i did that quick fall in love

she didnt love me she said in the name of a clean break
she wouldnt go to places we shared and i wonder
what that means for protests

like can we overcome being awkward to protest

DO THE RIGHT THING

theres no way it doesnt end

                  in violence

CLASSIC SONNET
for paul

the trees are breathing life again into
      the orange sky which needs something to fill
it up like big balloons. some mountain dew
      could wake us up (although a sketchy pill
would fill that need as well). some folks just know
      how to apply the golden rule at times
when rhythm and pentameter lack glow
      & the outside is barren, therefore, rhymes

become preferred, metaphor-ically.
      paul, you goof so well; you never need to
& still your laughs immerse. "genially"
      is a word ive heard used to describe you
&/or your general affectations. please
      leave us without eager. Not without ease.

APPLE
sonnet in which the sky and sky hopinka have my back

ah the sun is squeezin all the pink and purple out
of it all im worried therell be none left

for tomorrow what do i know! the sky again in my poems
all the time cause so much time spent lookin at the sky

so sue me, sky! youre already all around me
plus sky hopinka has my back

ah when you and sky meet itll be a trip
olivia i want to fall asleep in the proximity of your shoulder

i do not like the lack of sleep
in a bed not yours i do not like much of it with you not here

dont get it twisted i am generally happy like when you buy an apple
and then it tastes like an apple

anyway now i got no love for distance nor time keeping us
apart like this i wish the car wreck outside crashing was us instead of them

I DREAMT YOU WERE DEAD

and when i woke up the first thing i saw wasnt
the scribble of your hair on a pillow or your bodys

elevator breathing up and down snoozing but
incredibly a big round moon right at the top

of the window i just happened to be turned towards

i was bereft you were dead and now
neither of us are those things

sometimes poems are too obvious

you are the moon of course and i am the dream
having had it and then awaking to you as i have

but if you are the moon can i be the earth
our distance so big our gravity so necessary

HAVE MERCY

ive gotten a lot
of mileage out
of the luxuries

of slaughter i
swerved to hit
a collapsed bird

on the road today
im not sure if it
was already dead

or not but it certainly
couldnt fly it was
a puddle of a bird

meanwhile several police
officers stood outside
an indoor

soccer field staring off
into the distance
with their guns pointed

at a coyote one of them
shot at it but it didnt
move the damn thing

was frozen they shot
more at it it
continued to wag its tail mockingly

i dont know much
about my family history
but i have a little blue

card i carry that says im tsaligi
so i

often feel displaced

eventually the youngest
of the gathered officers
got sent over

to the animal and discovered
it was a scarecrow
with a couple of bullet holes

in its ass today
the news said
that fifty terrorist attacks

were prevented through
the surveillance of hundreds
of thousands of americans

which i saw careening across a screen
displaying the news in a restaurant
while i was eating

lunch todays featured picture
on wikipedia is
an albatross i admire

the brazen irony
of secrets a few
of the officers

had missed and put
thumbsized holes
in the dirt so

there were ants scurrying
about confusedly which
come to think of it

is pretty much how ants

always seem to get around
i bet

they have a better plan
than they get credit for
weve all got a little

torture in our blood
but its a matter of what side
our ancestors were on

mine are on both
i never got
any money from the government

for being tsaligi
but thats the first thing
people ask me

when they find out
it was so cold
in the airconditioned

restaurant i felt
uncomfortable but then
it was so hot

outside that i didnt want
to be there
either most of us

have mercy every now
and again
i dont

look tsaligi
except maybe
the nose a bit

i dont look like
much of anything
i cant remember the last time

i looked in the mirror i hate having
my picture
taken

MMMBOP

fuck the whole universe
is coming out of me as i breathe and
comes back in when i breathe in i wish

hanson said an mmmbop is a unit of time

i should have bought those $3 cigarettes at the gas station but
i am trying to quit i am trying in a general sense

i keep thinking people are people from other parts of my life
like i see someone in kansas city at hy vee
and think they are a poet who lives in bellingham

i think i am just lonely and a bit sad

the sun is starting to stay out a bit longer
its going to be in the fifties this weekend
the royals home opener is in like five weeks
spring is coming i guess i mean

i want to breathe and smell leaf not cold

mmmbop is playing from a playlist i made for soham
who had a goodbye party in a planetarium or something
ngoho hosted and i was going to dj and i dont know i was depressed

but also sick but also sad and i bled on a suit i was going to wear
to see soham off but i didnt want to so i dont know i just stayed home

SEEMS LIKE FOREVER AGO
sonnet

what am i going to do if you die

      might be green outside if you die

            might wonder did i say everything
     i wanted to say near your small ears

           sierra you will die but probably after me
                         i mean cmon

when we sleep we talk

when we sleep we walk the del taco wrapper streets
       and catch the bus and try to read what is going
on in the graffiti which is cheaper than the newspaper

and my skeleton wants to jump out onto the tracks
                        in some extravagant way to say hey
         sierra look at me! sierra! sierra!
               what do you think!

EYE BELIEVE

the sun gravity that there can be a person out there for anyone that sleep is
necessary that three meals a day is what you gotta do hydration that there is
someone beautiful waiting for me when i get home that i am always thinking of
her that i have a mother who loves me that i am safe that i am trusted that i do a
little bit better every day that kanye went off the rails but his old records still
slap that i buy too much food that the sky is often lovely that i am not in nature
enough that recycling is important that money isnt really real that the systems
seem too big but poems like this can take them down

the stares arent always fair but i dare you to find yourself amongst the shelves
when you feel unseen you think how can they treat me

pink purple lavender eggshell white mayonnaise yellow green jade midnight
blue kind of blue navy blue orange burnt orange white black burnt sienna cyan
turquoise magenta rose hot pink sunny day cheez-it orange powerade orange
red gold

you can go out and take your voice and say something about it

i peer through the glass
inward and outward

i often think of
what i would be like
if i were someone else

a cloud screams across
the sky which is blue for now

im so in love
and thrilled for virnette too
two teachers in love

if we never walked i might have never been born
would i give up myself for my people
no trail of tears might mean no me but more us a tradeoff
i am content to live or not exist with
a small haven of tsaligi life still happily existing no canned foods
fresh deer meat and the three sisters and fresh water plenty
of sun and matriarchy

it is about me it is not about me i am myself but i am also them
i am what is and what could have been and what will be tsaligi

SO WHAT

what if i never met olivia
what if we never walked
what if we werent so fucking kind and or ignorant
what if my dad died from substance abuse
what if my mom died today
what if six shit on the floor
what if i never learn how to clean up after myself
what if i could never hear music
what if the debt collectors come after me
what if it comes back
what if i have another
what if i dont ever have another
what if olivia gets pregnant
what if she never does
what if my destiny and your legacy are tied together (kwabena)
what if there was no more water
what if we learned a language beyond violence
what if violence is the only language
what if my love for olivia is so strong it changes the world
what if i stop using plastic
what if i stop getting fast food
what if i take a nap
what if my poems are strong but could be stronger
what if my poems are strong
what if kanye didnt get so weird
what if i cut sugar and salt out of my diet
what if i go grey
what if the world was more beautiful because i pushed it that way
what if I stop eating fast food

ideally i would have a garden i eat out of mostly
maybe raise some chickens but then
id have to learn how to kill

the chicken i eat right now is from somewhere
i dont know killed by someone i dont know
given to me by someone i dont know

i like listening to sports radio in the drivethru
sometimes when i feel lonely i go to the drivethru
even if i am not hungry it makes me feel good
to be amongst the people in their cars

FREEDOM IS (THE FUTURE LOOKS LIKE)

we are our ancestors wildest dreams
thats what virnette said anyway and then she said
she heard it from someone else
this is a poem in nineteen lines for juneteenth

its clints birthday today we facetimed during my lunch break
he seemed happy

i just stretched and my bones popped
its hot and im tired

its hot! im tired! you can see it in my eyes

i hope the sault record helps me stay up and pray up

i read some frank ohara to vanessa today
then we watched him read having a coke with you
i shared my screen it felt very intimate for two people
whove never met face to face

i am happier than ive ever been, i told duggan yesterday
i said wow in every way im fulfilled
i dont even care if its hot
im alive and so are you
and that is beautiful

LIFE

ELEGY
for k.s.

the last time i saw you you
were naked under a streetlight

now youre permanent naked
under a permanent streetlight

cremation makes sense

the slop of all bodies turned
to incredible nothing

every time i take a clumsy sip
of water in bed i think of you openchested
hot july

(it really could have been 13 years ago to the day)

sloppily drinking a beer letting it spill
over your chest and saying

ah
it just feels so nice
the cold
thats the best part of it

POEM TO BE READ ON A LOOP
sonnet

there is no how

like olivia

it all starts with you

to you as far

so hold all the power therein

as i can

are the beginning and

fathom which

like you

to be fair

as the big bang

is not much at all

of you its like of you   i think of you all the time sometimes

when i think

OLIVIA

sort of some sort of impossibly permanent like desire
the opposite of death more like a flower
reaching up towards the sun or
the way a can of soda hisses happily at you
knowing youre about to drink it

sort of some sort of like the ground
is there but not really youre walking on something pleasantly
spongy but still steady as if you could walk with certainty
on one of those moon bounces that children
of well-to-do parents have
at their ninth birthday parties

sort of some sort of a hand jutting out
from the opposite of a grave reaching for sleepy breathing
in the darkest part of the evening

sort of some sort of feeling that your heart
is a mixing bowl getting filled up with all kinds
of ingredients some familiar some not so much the trust
it will all turn out fine in fact better

sort of some sort of sound of pure joy the sound
of the body the sound of goofy intonations a secret
language developed and maintained

sort of some sort of language of two bodies

sort of some sort of no way to say it really
its beyond what can be said

OLIVIA
sestina

stuck in one body
my heart
beats and belongs
blood and rhythm together
mine becoming our
need to wash the dishes

our dishes
scraping food off them to clean off your body
of work which made our
dinner which might clog my heart
all the meat potatoes carrots together
as though they belong

time without you does be long
crust evolves upon the dish
of my heart which is not together
or with it or whatever my body
via my heart
thumps oddly and wishes for an our

maybe to sit around and watch an R
rated movie where no one belongs
to the part they play theyre all too beautiful making art
for popcorn enjoyment a big aluminum dish
full of dead kernels their bodies
reduced to little tan husks at least they were together

when they were enjoyed we strived to gather
our
body
of popcorn work the kernels belonged
to the aluminum bowl which hit the dishes
to be cleaned the butter made our hearts

work overtime my eyes and heart
work overtime whenever we step out of the shower together
clean like new dishes
bodies each others but also our

own belonging
together our bodies

you know i hate to dish but highkey my heart
pines to smack itself out my body when were together
our future hanging out assured it will spread it will be long

OLIVIA
sonnet, last poem written for the book, 7/1/2021

this morning
i spilled salsa
on the floor

and didnt see it
olivia cleaned it up

i never see the messes i make
until its too late

thank you for listening
and reading

thank you for everything

you are important
you are wonderful

please keep spreading beauty
like the sunset spreads its colors

EXIT SURVEY
21 questions

A microphone
lowers itself down into the shot? This
is all a bad

movie?
We were never
alive anyway? Good

news? The unmistakable air of whatever
exhaled every few words from the KC
cop with the bad luck

to address the press?
The anchorman coming alive?
Dum-da dums

of breaking news? Did we dream
our first kisses?
Hellos? Snow

it now appears never fell? The feet
we rested our feet upon mid-dream? We
never were? Some kid

just picked up his dog's shit? And
left it in our neighbor's trashcan? Should
I have gone after him? Stopped

him? Plan on floating through this
being real, knowing my long sighs
are someone

else's? Not
bothering to call anyone? About
the gunshots going off? Down the block? In celebration?

ACKNOWLEDGMENTS

These poems sample "The Star-Spangled Banner" by Francis Scott-Key, "Groovin'" by the Young Rascals, FIGURE OUT WHO TRANSLATED THIS VERSION OF *The Iliad* by Homer, "The Trees" by Philip Larkin, Roger Goodell's 2017 NFL Draft announcement of the selection of Patrick Mahomes II, "MMMBop" by Hanson, "Stay Up, Pray Up" by SAULT, "Itchycoo Park" by the Small Faces, "21 Questions" by 50 Cent feat. Nate Dogg.

Versions of some included poems have appeared in *Outlook Springs*, *Matter: A Journal of Political Poetry*, *Yellow Medicine Review*, and AT LEAST ONE ANTHOLOGY YOU NEED TO LOOK UP. ALSO PROBABLY SOME OTHER PUBLICATIONS YOU DON'T RECALL.

GV to Mom, Olivia, Freddy, Paul, Ed, the 7-11 on Linwood and Gillham, and Woodland Pattern Book Center.

This work generally owes a debt to *The Beatles' Second Album*.

Answers to "Exit Survey" should be mailed to VA Poetry, 643 S. 2nd St., MKE, WI 53204 or emailed to comments@whitehouse.gov.

Franklin K.R. Cline is an enrolled member of the Cherokee Nation and the author of *So What* (VA-11). He lives in Kansas City with Six and Olivia.

He teaches English at the Frontier School of Excellence.

CPSIA information can be obtained
at www.ICGtesting.com
Printed in the USA
LVHW041803151121
703328LV00003B/79